Help Your Dog Be Eager To Listen To You

The Only Method You'll Ever Need For Your Perfectly Behaved Dog

Help Your Dog Be EagerTo Listen To You is a work of my own creation.

The information in this book was correct at the time of publication, and the Author does not assume any liability for loss or damage caused by errors or omissions, again, this is my perspective, opinion, and experience, so it has been written as such.

ISBN - 978-1-961185-56-2

Cover, Book Design, and Layout by Kim Hawkinson
On Point Dog Training LLC
www.onpointdogtraining.com

www.inomniaparatuspublishing.com

This book is dedicated to all of the badass dog parents helping their dogs live their best lives possible.

Table of Contents

Introduction

Hello, amazing dog parent!

I am thrilled that you are opening this book!

Before you get started, let me introduce myself. My name is Kim Hawkinson and my specialty is helping dogs learn to control their emotional states. This means helping them learn to be calm and not get triggered, as well as learn that they're safe not having those reactions to things.

What goes along with that is also listening to their parents so that they can be trusted to go places, do all the things, and have all the adventures with us so we can make lasting memories together.

I believe each dog is a soul and personality, and that our dogs want to make us happy. It's up to us to show them what we expect from them and teach them how to treat us in order for those things to happen.

1

Getting back to the book....

You reading this means you're ready to have your dog listening better so you can live a better life with them.

> *Even if you've thought of your dog as "just a dog", I'm here to tell you that they are so much more, and are much more intelligent than we silly humans give them credit for.*

This book is going to explain all of the exact steps I take all of my clients through, even those who spend thousands of dollars on training.

The first five sections will each talk about a component of helping your dog make the

choice to WANT to listen to you better. The last part of the book will explain how everything ties together so you can start getting the dog of your dreams as soon as possible!

This book will not tell you how to teach individual behaviors or solve specific issues you're having with your dog. Instead, it will teach you the system for how to get your dog to listen.

Each section will have Pro-Trainer Insights that will shed light on very important pieces of information for you to keep in mind as you're working with your dog and maximize your results.

After each section, you'll find actionable steps, as well as worksheets where you can jot down notes for yourself on how you want to train your dog.

Now, if you're thinking to yourself,

"But my dog is already a really good dog. They already do everything they're supposed to at home"

I have a question for you:

Is your pup doing everything on autopilot or are they actually listening?

If you asked them to do something they might not want to do....

Would they do it?

If you're unsure, keep reading.

Don't feel the need to rush through the book.

Do each step so you can implement the training and experience doing each step.

It's important to note, the steps in this book aren't difficult. They're just different from what you've done before, or are currently doing.

Your dog wants your guidance and leadership. Your dog wants to make you happy.

Remember to have fun and enjoy the ride 😄 I'm so incredibly excited to hear of your success!

Expectations

This is the first part of really making sure that we set our dogs up for as much success when it comes to them listening to us.

When you know what you are wanting in any situation with your dog, you increase the likelihood of not being disappointed and getting what you want from them.

When I say the word expectations, I'm talking about what you are expecting from your dog when you ask them to do something. This includes what you want your dog to be doing with their body. This means how quickly you want your dog to do the behavior you asked them to do, and how long to perform that behavior. This includes the emotional state you want them in when you ask behavior as well.

The more specific you can be with your expectations the better.

Let's look at a human example for a moment:

- You're about to go out with someone and you're incredibly excited about it. You've done everything to make sure you look fantastic and you're ready to hit the town.

- You expect from the date that the person tells you you look great, have wonderful conversations over food or during your outing with them, and you also expect to have the person want to get together again if you have a good time.

Going along with what you are expecting, you can also look at what you're NOT expecting.

- You're not expecting the other person to be checking out other people while you're with them on the date.

- You're not expecting your date to be rude, crass, or straight-up creepy on your date.

- You're not expecting your date to take you to an inappropriate or vulgar location.

(It seems I've thought a lot about what I DON'T want in a partner!)

You get the drift.

It's the same for our dogs. If you know what you're looking for, you can continue encouraging that behavior.

If you get something that you don't like or fall outside of those expectations, you can shut it down ASAP and help your dog do something different.

It's important to note that your expectations have two requirements:

1. These expectations are for you and your life. Joe-shmoe famous dog trainer can tell you all day long that you need this and that for your dog but if that doesn't go along with, or align, with your lifestyle, you and your dog don't need it.

2. These expectations are for you and your life. Joe-shmoe famous dog trainer can tell you all day long that you need this and that for your dog but if that doesn't go along with, or align, with your lifestyle, you and your dog don't need it.

Pro-Trainer Insight: Know what you want but don't be so attached to what things look like or how your dog does them, as long as your dog does them. Our dogs aren't robots and they need space to figure things out

With all that in mind, next, we're going to talk about the four most important words to use when directing your dog to do the things.

Here is a training video I did
talking about expectations

Join my Private Facebook Community
where I talk about expectations
and other dog related topics

Actionable Step

Fill in the Expectations worksheet and get really clear on what you're wanting to see from your dog when you tell them to do something.

When you're clear on what you want, you'll also be clear on what you don't want and can use the negative work (next section) to stop your dog and get them on the right path.

Expectations

What behaviors do you want your dog to be able to do or better at?

What do you want your do to do in certain situations or certain areas in your home?

What are your expectations for those behaviors or situations?

_____

_____

_____

_____

_____

_____

_____

_____

_____

_____

_____

_____

_____

_____

_____

_____

_____

_____

Expectations

Expectations

The Four Most Important Words

Everything we want from our dogs and the relationships we have with them starts with communication.

There's communication with our words as well as communication with our bodies. We'll get into the body language later but for now, we're working with our words.

Dogs are simple creatures, not to be confused with unintelligent. Our dogs can troubleshoot and problem-solve. Despite what some might think, they are incredibly intelligent.

Pro-Trainer Insight: When you tell your dog about something, whether it be a word, an object, a sound, or any other thing, you give them power over that thing because they understand that thing better than they did before.

When we want to guide them and know how to do something, we need to keep the guidance simple. In addition to that, we also need to give these words meaning so our dogs clearly understand them.

We will go over the four most important words, as well as how to give that word meaning below:

Word #1: The Reward Word

You can use the word "Good" or "Yes" as your reward word. This tells your dog that what they're doing is exactly what you're wanting and they're going to get paid for doing it.

For rewards, you can use:

- Food or Treats
- Love, Affection, or Scratches
- Toys
- Play
- Or anything else that your dog finds valuable

To give the word meaning (a.k.a.: to shape the word):

Say the word and immediately give the reward. This lets your dog know that what they are doing is good and to continue to do things that result in them hearing the reward word.

Word #2: The Negative Word

You can use the word "No" for this word. This lets our dogs know that what they are doing will not get them the reward.

To give this word meaning, simply say the word "No" and help your dog do something else (if you're just starting to train a behavior). If you've already been working on a behavior and your dog already knows it, after you say "No", give them a moment to see if they can troubleshoot.

Don't feel the need to rush in and help them fix it. Give them a few seconds to fix it themselves before you go into save the day.

Word #3: The Reinforcing Word

To decide which word to use for this specific word purpose, you can use the alternate word from the reward word. So, if you used "Yes" for your reward, you can use the word "Good" for the reinforcing word. You can also use the words "Wait" or "Close".

You use this word to let your dog know that they're doing a great job but they're not quite done yet with what you asked them to do. You would use this to expand on a behavior that your dog already knows. This word comes before the reward word.

An example would be:

You're wanting to expand on the amount of time your dog is sitting after you say the command.

You would say the reinforcing word and then the reward word to let your dog know that one follows the other.

To give the word meaning, you would say the reinforcing word and immediately say the reward word right after. This lets your dog know that after they hear the reinforcing word, the reward is coming.

It stops your dog from getting frustrated or irritated that they're continuing to wait with no end to the behavior in sight.

As you progress, you can put more time in between the reinforcing word and reward word. You can say the reinforcing word as many times as you want in the beginning and start to decrease the number of times

you say it as you progress with your dog, and they start to understand what you are wanting from them.

Word #4: The Release Word

This word tells your dog they're done doing the thing you asked them to do. You can use the word "Done" or "Free" for the release word.

This word is important because it tells our dogs when they're done doing a behavior. It stops them from stopping the behavior on their own and doing what they want after you ask for a behavior.

To give the word meaning, say the word and then initiate movement from them. You could stand in front of them, say your release word, and then pat your legs, calling them to you.

You could also ask them to sit, say your release word and then toss a treat, and tell them they can go get it.

Pro-Trainer Insight: It doesn't matter what words you decide to use as long as you use them consistently. (This is why some  people speak to their dogs in different languages like German, Spanish, and French).

The main point of giving this word meaning is that you want to see your dog moving.

In the next section, we'll talk about setting some rules and boundaries for your dog.

Join my Private Facebook Community
where I talk about expectations
and other dog related topics

Here is a training video I did
talking about The Four Most
Important Words

Actionable Step

Talk with anyone else that's in the house and pick your words together. Make sure that everyone understands what each words mean so everyone is on the same page.

Sidenote: Involving the kiddos help these words will allow them to have ownership of the words and get them excited to use them

Four Most Important Words

What words do you want to use for each of the Most Important Words?

Remember, if your native language isn't English, there's another language spoken in your home, or you want your dog to only listen to you, use words from other languages.

Reward Word:

_____

Negative Word:

_____

Reinforcing Word:

_____

Release Word:

_____

Any other words and what you want them to mean:

_____

_____

_____

_____

_____

Four Most Important Words

Are there any other words that you want to mean specific things? (Ex. I know a cat owner who taught her cat to go away when she said the words F*#! Off. To each their own 😂)

Four Most Important Words

Rules & Boundaries

When people hear the words, rules and boundaries, they generally think of restrictions and withholding things. When it comes to our dogs and creating rules and boundaries, it's so important to remember that our dogs live by rules.

There's a reason that in a dog pack, there's a dog that has the job of "alpha". The alpha creates all the rules that the rest of the pack lives by. Who has which job? Where does which animal sleep? Who's allowed to go where? Who's allowed to eat what? The list goes on and on as there are endless rules to create within a community.

If you stop and think about it, we live our lives by rules as well.

When you see a red light in your car, you know exactly what you're supposed to do.

When you see a line of people when you go into the bank, you know you're supposed to get behind the last person in that line in order to get helped.

These are just the simple rules and guidelines that we live our lives by so everything works in an orderly manner. Creating rules and boundaries does the exact same thing for our dogs.

> *The vast majority of the reason our dogs get reactive, meaning they start barking, or get fearful, stressed, or anxious, is fear of the unknown. This world was not made with our dogs in mind*

As our children grow up, we tell them what sounds are, what objects are, and what is expected of them when we go places together.

Some kids are still fearful of loud or sharp noises as they grow up, but they learn that those loud noises won't cause them pain or injury and learn to be ok with them. They know what to expect.

Rules and boundaries do the exact same thing for our dogs.

So how do we set these rules and boundaries? I'm glad you asked.

Think about how you want your dog to be acting in certain situations.

What do you want them to do when you tell them to sit?

How long do you want them to remain in that seated position?

Are they allowed to do the butt swivel where they remain sitting but swivel around to face another direction on their booty?

Are they allowed in the kitchen when you're cooking?

If so, how close are they allowed to get close to you in the kitchen?

If not, where is the barrier your dog isn't allowed to cross?

Where's the line between the kitchen and the rest of your house your dog needs to stay behind?

Does that make sense?

Expectations and Rules are very closely linked. Think of expectations as the things you want to see from your dog, and rules boundaries as the expectations for your dog's emotional state and using their self-control.

I'll be going over some tools to help you teach your dog these rules and guidelines in the Tools section.

Next, we're going to talk about resources and how to get your dog to WANT to listen consistently.

Join my Private Facebook Community
where I talk about expectations
and other dog related topics

Here is a training video I did
talking about Rules

Actionable Step

Think of how you want your dog to act or behave in certain situations.

Are there any areas inside or outsde of the house where you want them to behave in a certain way?

Make note of all of those on the next pages.

Rules & Boundaries

What are some situations where you want your dog to exercise self-control and calmness?

How do you want your dog to act, or what are the things you want them to do in those situations? (Think of this is an extension of the Expectations Sheet)

Rules & Boundaries

Rules & Boundaries

Resources

Resources are the things that your dog place value on. And the kicker is that we don't get to decide what our dogs value.

Pro-Trainer Insight: We don't get to decide what our dogs place value on. There are the external things that our dogs value like  food, treats, and toys. There are also the intrinsic things, the non-physical things, that make our dogs FEEL good.

Some dogs love ice cubes.

Some dogs love playing with blankets.

My dog will practically do my taxes for an empty toilet paper roll to tear apart.

I don't question it but I use that thing she puts value in, that resource, to ask her to do the things I need her to do.

We go to a job and get a paycheck every week or two weeks, right? The resource in that example would be money.

Controlling the resources is never a reason to withhold anything from your dog. It's a way to give them more of the things they value and make them happy because they prioritize listening to you rather than listening to themselves and their own rules.

Resources are what we pay our dogs with when we use the Reward Word we talked about earlier.

Examples of resources to take control of include (but are not limited to):

- Food
- Treats
- Toys
- Raised Surfaces like couches where they're super comfy
- Their freedom and space around them (we talk about how to take control of this in the Tool section)
- And, again, anything our dogs put value in

Pro-Trainer Insight: Controlling the resources is never a reason to withhold anything from your dog. It's a way to give them more of the things they value and make them happy because they prioritize listening to you rather than listening to themselves and their own rules.

Join my Private Facebook Community where I talk about expectations and other dog related topics

Here is a training video I did talking about Resources

Actionable Step

Make a list of the obvious resources you can easily take control of when it comes to your pup.

After, make a list of the things that your dog puts value in, the things that they specifically love. (Think of my dog Harlow doing my taxes for the empty toilet paper roll )

Resources

What are the things that your dog views as positive that you can use to reward them?

Remember, think of things that you can touch that your dog values, as well as the things that make them feel amazing like life rewards (going for a walk or a car ride)

Resources

46

Tools To Use

Now we get the good stuff when it comes to getting our dogs to listen. Do yourself and your dog a favor and read the Pro-Trainer Insight.

Pro-Trainer Insight: Your dog needs to do the work, not you. You pulling your dog with a leash, pushing them back behind the boundary you set earlier, or holding them down to stop them from jumping is you doing the work, not your dog.

So often we think that our dogs aren't capable of things but that's because we don't know how to not do the work for our dogs. We don't know how to help them learn to use their own self-control.

My favorite tool to use with a dog is a leash.

A leash helps us humans keep control over a situation, gives our dogs the space to figure things out for themselves, and troubleshoot the situation in front of them.

A leash allows us to keep our dogs close to us when we need to, as well as take control of their freedom when they decide they'd rather throw their butt up in the air and not listen when we know they know better.

Use a leash to help control your dog's freedom when you need them to be calmer, more still in certain situations, or, again, not move towards something.

When there comes a time when you need to use the leash to get your dog to move or

start to pull them, I want you to use what's called leash pressure. Leash pressure is when you start to pull on the leash but rather than making your dog move with the pull of the leash itself, you give enough pressure to make it a little uncomfortable for your dog to remain stationary wherever they are.

When your dog does give in to the pressure and starts moving forward, that is when you release the pressure because your dog, at that point, is doing what you want them to do which is move forward.

When you're working with your dog, everything is a give-and-take. Any type of confrontational or uncomfortable pressure like leash pressure must go away when our dogs start doing the work themselves.

Another of my favorite tools to use with dogs is spatial pressure. Spatial pressure is when we use our dog's own personal space bubble to our advantage and help them move back when they move out of a position that we want them to be in.

Imagine you're on a busy sidewalk with a lot of people. The people on the right are going in one direction, and the people on the left are going in the opposite direction, just like cars on a road.

As you're walking on the right side, you see a person walking in the opposite direction switch lanes and start walking directly towards you.

What is eventually going to happen is you will either move around the person walking towards you, or you will stop moving forward and begin to move backward because that person is now invading your space.

That is spatial pressure.

> *Our dogs are incredibly adaptable, which means that they're really good at figuring out the loopholes and gray areas to get what they want.*

When you're using spatial pressure, feel free to use your outstretched hands to make yourself bigger. You may need to move from side to side, and you may need to step into your dog's personal space to help them move backward.

Just like with the leash pressure, when your dog has moved back or stopped moving forward and they're in the location that you want them to remain in, stop giving the pressure and allow your dog to figure things out on their own.

If your dog stays still for a moment, and then starts to move again, you give spatial pressure again. Using spatial pressure is helping dogs figure out that the gray areas and loopholes are no longer present.

Next we're going to talk about how to put everything we've talked about together!

Join my Private Facebook Community where I talk about expectations and other dog related topics

Here is a training video I did talking about dog training tools (there's an extra bonus added in there for you!

Actionable Step

What tools would you like to use when you're working with your dog.

This is Important: You have to be comfortable using that tool. Don't listen to the in-the-moment YouTube trainer that says "You must be using this thing!"

You have to KNOW how to use the tool and you have to be comfortable using it.

Tools

What are some tools that you can use with your dog that will allow you to help them better understand what you're wanting from them?

Also, think of situations that you can start to incorporate these tools in. You can use a leash inside as well as out, and that goes for all other tools.

Tools

Putting Everything Together

Now it's time to put everything that we've talked about together and paint the picture of your perfectly behaved dog.

First, set your expectations for what you want your dog to do when you ask them to do something.

Next, you're going to set your rules and boundaries that you want your dog to follow and listen to.

Next, you use your four most important words to direct your dog to be able to fulfill those expectations and follow the rules and boundaries you set for them.

You use the resources that your dog finds valuable to reward them when they do the correct thing that you want them to continue doing.

You use the tools that were mentioned to help your dog not just understand what you are wanting, but have them do the work themselves rather than you feeling you have to micro-manage and always stay on top of your dog's actions.

And that is how you put all of the tools we've talked about to create your perfectly behaved pup!

Moving Forward

So what are you waiting for?

Go start working with your dog so you can have a better-behaved companion, so you can start having people over at your home, or you can start having more adventures with your dog, taking them with you and creating more lasting memories with them.

It's important to remember that there are no cut-in-stone behaviors your dog has to know. There are no cut-in-stone ways to teach a behavior either.

Your journey with your dog is your own and you both get to enjoy it working together.

Don't compare where you are with someone who has been training and working with their dog for years, or with a professional you see on YouTube.

As you work together more, you'll notice what your dog likes to do, as well as what they don't like to do.

You'll notice their personality coming out more, as well as their curiosity about the world around them.

Enjoy this time together and make the most of it.

Show your dog some love today and I'll talk to you soon

Actionable Step

Put together everything you've learned in this book.

Don't feel like you have to rush things. What you're about to implement is new and what's more important than implementing everything fast, is implementing everything effectively so your dog understands what you're wanting and what the new rules of the house are.

Resources

My Private Facebook Community

Be My Friend On Facebook

Here's A List of All My Links Where You Will Find Freebies, Resources, and All Types of Events I Have Going On

**You can go through and add all of the videos from the sections in a playlist on YouTube